HIDEY HOLES

*Beautiful Hideaways, Bolt Holes & Harbours
in England & Wales*

ROBIN WHITCOMB

Copyright © 2016 Robin Whitcomb

The moral right of the author has been asserted.

Apart from any fair dealing for the purposes of research or private study, or criticism or review, as permitted under the Copyright, Designs and Patents Act 1988, this publication may only be reproduced, stored or transmitted, in any form or by any means, with the prior permission in writing of the publishers, or in the case of reprographic reproduction in accordance with the terms of licences issued by the Copyright Licensing Agency. Enquiries concerning reproduction outside those terms should be sent to the publishers.

Matador
9 Priory Business Park,
Wistow Road, Kibworth Beauchamp,
Leicestershire. LE8 0RX
Tel: 0116 279 2299
Email: books@troubador.co.uk
Web: www.troubador.co.uk/matador
Twitter: @matadorbooks

ISBN 978 1785890 642

British Library Cataloguing in Publication Data.
A catalogue record for this book is available from the British Library.

Printed and bound in Malta by Gutenberg Press Ltd
Typeset in 12pt Bembo by Troubador Publishing Ltd, Leicester, UK

Matador is an imprint of Troubador Publishing Ltd

This book is in memory of my dear old Labrador 'Coco'. Over the past five years she has followed me faithfully to every 'Hidey Hole' in the book – from the rugged coastal paths of South West Cornwall to the majestic castles of Northumberland in North East England.

CONTENTS

About the Author	vi
Introduction	vii
The West Country	1
Cornwall	1
South Devon	25
North Devon	33
Wales	41
The North of England	51
East Anglia	63
Artist's Acknowledgements	71
Further Acknowledgements	72

ABOUT THE AUTHOR

Robin Whitcomb was born in Scarborough, Yorkshire in 1945. He was educated at Cranleigh School in Surrey. After leaving school, Robin spent two years in America working in the oil business in Tulsa, Oklahoma. He then went to Hollywood, California to meet up with his older brother Ian who was enjoying enormous success with his smash record 'You Turn Me On'. Ian introduced Robin to rising stars Sonny and Cher and he became their drummer and percussionist playing on their big hit 'I Got You Babe'.

Returning to the UK, Robin played cricket for the MCC and for Richmond Rugby Club for 10 years. While at St Luke's College, Exeter he represented the SW Counties XV v South Africa and then Fiji. He also played county rugby for Devon and Surrey. Robin worked for The Daily Telegraph before teaching at Dulwich Prep, London for thirty three years. He has been coaching cricket at Colet Court, St Paul's Junior School in London for the past eight years.

This is Robin's third book following firstly 'Wealding The Willow' - a picture portrait of village cricket in the Weald' (published by Tempus in 2005) and then 'Home Sweet Home - the most unusual places and homes where people live' (published by Troubador in 2011). Robin lives overlooking the River Wey in a converted paper mill in Surrey. He has two sons, Patch 30 and Beanie 29.

INTRODUCTION

When putting together my last picture book 'Home Sweet Home - most unusual places where people live in England and Wales' (Troubador Publishing}, I discovered clusters of remote beautiful little villages around the England and Wales coastline and this gave me the idea of putting together a new picture book. So, once again, I packed my bags and loaded the chocolate Labrador dog Coco into the car to return to these eye-catching coastline hideaways, havens and harbours.

In this book it was additionally encouraging for me to include paintings by local artists who live close to the tucked-away places I visited. It was a chance to vary the styles of the artists– some using oils, some watercolours, one or two etchings and the gouache technique of Richard Tuff ('Flushing Pier'– pictured left). I do hope that you will have as much pleasure reading this book as I have had in producing it.

The West Country
CORNWALL

CADGWITH

It is no wonder that, for over a century, thousands of artists have been attracted to this quaint tiny harbour squeezed into a narrow valley.

Overlooking the compact beach on the slopes of the valley are pretty thatched cottages made of local stone with cob walls (pictured bottom right).

Once down in this characteristic Cornish fishing village, a collection of various fishing vessels can be seen resting upon the shingle beach at low tide. Behind these stand the old cellars, lofts and capstan houses.

Cadgwith owes its existence to the fishing industry. Pilchard fishing was prolific in the 1900's.

At that time local men who were appointed as 'lookouts' were posted on the headlands in the attempt to spot large shoals of pilchards.

These 'lookouts' were known as 'huers' because when they caught sight of the pilchards they shouted to the fishermen in their Cornish tongue 'Hewa Hewa' meaning 'Here they are!'

Nowadays pilchard fishing has given way to catching crabs, lobsters, monkfish and conger eel. Most of the catch is sold abroad with the remainder in the hands of the local fishmonger.

MULLION COVE

Tucked away on the Lizard Peninsular in South Cornwall lies Mullion Cove. After years of pounding from southerly winter gales, a secure shelter was much needed. So finally the harbour was completed in 1895 with two sturdy sea walls protecting the cove.

In the early days smuggling and 'wrecking' was rife on the Cornish coast, and Mullion was no exception. Ships were lured onto the rocks by carefully placed 'warning' fires which were infested with 'wreckers'.

The harbour, owned by The National Trust since 1945, had a lifeboat station from 1867 until 1909. Today the old pilchard cellar and net store are still preserved.

Saint Mellanus Church dates back to the 13th century. The oak screen, restored in 1964, emanates back to the original carvings from the 15th century.

Mullion is blessed with a wide range of quality food ranging from roast sea bream to the traditional Cornish pasty.

'The devil' the local folk say 'will never venture across the Tamar River into Cornwall because, if he did, he'd be chopped up and put into a pasty!'

BOSCASTLE

Boscastle Harbour lies shielded behind vast towering cliffs. The harbour is unique because although it is mostly protective it can also be especially hostile in bad weather. In the past the North Cornwall coastline was notorious for being the graveyard for many ships seeking shelter from the force of the Atlantic gales.

The Harbour is full of attractive stone fishermen's cottages. One of the most unusual buildings is 'The Witchcraft Museum' (pictured below).

Boscastle had suffered from several floods in the past, but on the 16th of August 2004, the harbour was hit by the most extreme flash floods ever experienced in England (pictured below right). It was caused by the remnants of 'Hurricane Alex' which had crossed over the Atlantic.

The damage was extensive. A current of ten foot waves washed away seventy-five cars, five caravans and six buildings. A fleet of seven helicopters rescued one hundred and fifty young and elderly from the harbour.

MOUSEHOLE

Looking out towards St Michael's Mount across the bay, the little picture postcard harbour of Mousehole sits snuggly in front of narrow cobbled streets and stone-built fishermen's cottages.

'Mouzel', as it is pronounced, was Cornwall's leading fishing port for many years. The larger port of nearby Newlyn was developed in the 19th century and came to the forefront of the fishing industry.

The most important date in Mousehole's history is 1595 when the Spaniards landed in the harbour. They ransacked the village setting fire to all the houses.

The only house to survive belonged to Squire Jenkin Keigwin. Left on his own in Keigwin house (pictured far right), he managed to kill six Spaniards before he was shot – with his sword still in his hand.

Mousehole's history records two legendary characters. Dolly Pentreath (pictured far left) was an old lady who 'talked Cornish as readily as others do English.' She died in 1777 aged 101 and was thought to be the last person to speak her native Cornwall language. She was buried in the Parish of Paul Churchyard where a stone commemorates her distinction.

Tom Bawcock (pictured top left) was 'a Mousehole man through and through' and a heroic fisherman. The famous story of 'The Starry Gazy Pie' tells of Tom's brave venture onto the high seas in order to bring back a catch of fish in time for Christmas. Every year the Mousehole folk celebrate 'Tom Bawcock's Eve' on the 23rd December. The Ship Inn on the harbour front serves up 'The Starry Gazy Pie' which consists of seven sorts of fish baked under a crust with their heads coming up through the middle of the pie.

PORTHGWARRA

Hidden away, and only accessed by a very narrow country road winding down a steep valley, lies the enchanting little cove at Porthgwarra.

The slipway, built by local fishermen in 1880, leads down to a small sandy beach. It's a favourite summer haunt for children to play at low tide. To the left, at the bottom of the slip, is a tunnel approaching the beach (pictured right). The tunnel was drilled out by nearby St Just miners around 1890.

When the small sandy beach is covered at high tide, long shadows drape themselves across the formidable tower of boulders leading out to the Atlantic (pictured right).

Like most of Cornwall's coves, the scene can change very suddenly. In summertime at Porthgwarra the soft blue skies and sea are bathed in the evening sun. In sharp contrast the fierce winter storms pound relentlessly against the boulders.

Often banks of seaweed are blown onto the beach with the sand being shifted in the threatening gales. In recent times the picturesque cove of Porthgwarra has been used extensively in the BBC's production of 'Poldark'.

By the 1870's there were a dozen granite built houses existing in the small hamlet. Some families moved to Porthgwarra from other neighbouring coves because there was more chance of making a living fishing there.

In those early days the fishing boats only had the use of sails or oars. Navigating into the narrow cove needed considerable skill. In the 1890's records read: 'Shellfish dispatched from Porthgwarra – packed full in four carts and taken to the station destined for London.'

Today Porthgwarra is now almost a ghost hamlet in the winter months but, in the summer, discerning tourists will make sure they visit this unspoiled beautiful hideaway.

ZENNOR

Standing three hundred feet above sea level and less than a mile from the sea, Zennor takes its name from St Senara. The Norman church looks down over the tiny village. A memorial by the porch (pictured bottom right) commemorates John Davey, said to have been the last person to speak the ancient Cornish language as his native tongue. However, there is some question about this distinction because Dolly Pentreath, who died in Mousehole in 1777, is claimed to be credited with this honour.

The church of St Senara is best known for the Mermaid Chair. The medieval carving shows a mermaid with a mirror in one hand and a comb in the other. Adorning the chair is a colourful hand-woven cushion.

The story goes that the mermaid was enchanted by the voice of a chorister who, himself, had a fascination of the mermaid. He followed her down to the sea and the two were never to be seen again. Legend has it that sometimes they can be heard singing at night time.

Unlike the mermaid, another much more temporary inhabitant of Zennor was novelist D.H.Lawrence (pictured below). He and his wife Frieda stayed in the village from 1915 until 1917. Frieda was a cousin of the German ace pilot 'The Red Baron'. Rumours spread that the two were German spies and they were ordered to leave Cornwall.

FLUSHING

Across the Fal estuary, opposite the large port of Falmouth, lies picturesque Flushing. The colourful little village was named by Dutch engineers who were employed to build its quays and sea walls in the 17th Century.

The village became known as 'Little Falmouth' but Charles 11 agreed a ferry crossing from Falmouth allowing Flushing its own dependency and character. After centuries the ferry still makes the short crossing to and fro today (pictured below).

Some Queen Anne houses in Flushing were owned by captains of the Packet Ships docked in Falmouth. Sadly, after providing much employment, many of the Packet Ships were lost. Steam-powered vessels took over and the old Packet Ships became known as 'Coffin Ships'.

BOTALLACK MINE

Set up against the cliffs at Botallack, the remains of two engine houses make a dramatic foreground in front of the crashing waves of the deep blue Atlantic sea. The lower engine house was built in 1835 to pump water from the mine.

Botallack Mine is one of the most ancient hard-rock tin and copper mining areas in Cornwall. Miners – often father and son – worked many fathoms underground and in tunnels out under the sea in their attempt to break the ore.

The conditions were extremely dangerous but mining was the life-blood of the nearby St Just community (its church pictured) who depended on this ancient industry.

PENBERTH COVE

The National Trust, who have owned Penberth since 1957, described it as 'the most perfect of Cornish fishing coves.' It is tucked away at the end of a sheltered wooded valley on the Land's End Peninsular in South West Cornwall. One of the great advantages is that it is never crowded as there is only space for a few cars to park.

Traditions still remain as the fishermen put to sea in open boats – just as their fathers, their grandfathers and great grandfathers did ages and ages ago.

The fishing boats used to be dragged up by a horse drawn wheel and axel hoisting machine called a windlass. Larger craft used to be hauled from the sea by an unusual capstan that resembles a great cartwheel laid on its side (pictured below left).

Nowadays an electric winch is used to pull the boats up the granite slipway. Summer is the busiest time when the fishermen take their boats out at dawn, working their pots for lobsters, crawfish and crabs.

Fish are scarce in the winter time and the boats are pulled up high on the slipway – a safe haven from the gales that lash in towards this little idyllic cove.

17

CAPE CORNWALL

The tourist attraction of Land's End often distracts people from visiting the breath-taking views from its southerly close neighbour Cape Cornwall.

Until the first Ordnance Survey 200 years ago, it was thought that Cape Cornwall was the most westerly point in England.

The Brisons, the offshore rocks, are located just off Cape Cornwall (pictured below right). A monument stands high on top of the Cape cliffs (also pictured below). It commemorates the purchase of Cape Cornwall for all the Nation by H.J.Heinz and Company. The majority of the main headlands are owned by The National Trust.

GORRAN HAVEN

The sandy beach is overlooked by narrow village streets and alleyways.

On the left of this pretty little haven is a peninsula called 'Bodrugan's Leap'. It is believed that this is where Sir Henry Treworth of Bodrugan spurred his horse over the cliff to escape from his enemies in 1485 after supporting Richard 111's illfated cause at the Battle of Bosworth.

HELFORD

Enchanting thatched cottages with whitewashed walls and gardens adorned with colourful flowers make this idyllic backwater possibly the most eye-catching 'hidey hole' in England. It is hard to believe that hundreds of years ago, this sleepy haven was an important port where trading ships brought in French rum, tobacco and lace. The village was an anchorage for fishermen and coasters which transported Cornish tin.

Helford is one of seven creeks along the river – the best known is Frenchman's Creek immortalised by Daphne du Maurier's novel of the same name. Opposite Helford village on the north shore is the popular Ferryboat Inn (pictured below left) which dates back some 300 years. It is a nautical magnet and watering hole for all the yachting fraternity and can be reached by a ferry which dates back to the Middle Ages.

POLPERRO

Situated on the River Pol, this pretty well-informed village is one of the most attractive harbours in England. As far back as the 13th century it was known for its fishing.

Like many Cornish fishing villages, Polperro's pilchard fishing industry diminished in the early 20th century. Since the 1960's the fishing fleet search for flat fish, scallops, crabs and monkfish.

Polperro has a history of severe storms. One of the earliest was in 1774 when much of the harbour was destroyed. Fortunately a local benefactor paid a large sum of money for the repairs. 1817 produced another violent storm when 30 large boats and several houses were demolished. The worst recorded storm was in November 1824. Parts of the harbour were swept out to sea leaving fifty boats to be dashed to pieces.

Smuggling is believed to have prospered after Polperro was developed as a port in the 12th century. Much later, in the 18th century, a local merchant called Zephaniah Job, known as the 'Smugglers' Banker', schemed the importing of contraband such as spirits and tobacco from Guernsey in the Channel Islands. In order to prevent further smuggling, the coast guard service was introduced in the 19th century. The revenue officers patrolled the coast in search of smugglers and, when caught, the miscreants received stiff penalties.

Each summer Polperro attracts thousands of visitors. Nestling in a narrow combe of pretty whitewashed cottages are old fishing sheds mingled amongst craft shops, restaurants and elegant tea rooms (pictured below right).

After the hustle and bustle of the summer holiday season, Polperro reverts back to being the quiet little harbour village it always used to be a long, long time ago.

VERYAN

The little village of Veryan is probably best known for the round houses built during the Regency period around 1850-1870. The Reverend Jeremiah Trist was a notable figure in the parish and the houses were built for him. There were five of these round houses in the village all built with thatched roofs with a cross on top. The painting below is by the famous local artist Oliver Bedford (1902-1977).

Originally the buildings were known as 'Devil Proof' houses because the local folk thought that Satan could not hide in a house without corners. However there is little evidence of this and a much more convincing reason was that they were both attractive to look at and cheap to build.

The West Country
SOUTH DEVON

DITTISHAM

Standing high up, overlooking the widest part of the River Dart, is the attractive little village of Dittisham.

The view down to the shoreline is made up of a variety of yachts and other craft. In the middle of the village. at the bottom of a steep slope, is The Red Lion pub which was a coaching inn and dates back to 1750. Going back in time much further is St George's Church rebuilt in the early 14th century.

Navigating a well-known course across from Dittisham, the pedestrian ferry is a Godsend for passengers who wish to take the short boat trip across to Greenway Quay.

From the quayside it is only a short walk up through the woods to Greenway House standing high up overlooking the River Dart (pictured below).

The house is famous for being the home of the novelist Agatha Christie. As well as owning a number of properties in England, Agatha Christie lived at Greenway House from just before the Second World War until her death in 1976.

HOPE COVE

Heading west along the coastline from Salcombe towards Plymouth, lies the pretty little remote village of Hope Cove.

For much of its early life the secluded small harbour had a thriving fishing industry and, like many of its neighbours dotted along the Southwest coastline, there has been a history of smuggling.

Today the attractive little village, with its outer harbour wall still existing, has just a small community and there is a limited amount of fishing with the locals dependent on mainly crab and lobsters.

Hope Cove is made up of two diminutive hamlets – Inner Hope and Outer Hope.

At Inner Hope there is a collection of idyllic stone, cob and thatch cottages (pictured below). These very attractive homes, with colourful rose-clad walls and geraniums, form an eye-catching and quaint village square.

Outer Hope (pictured left) is just a brisk walk away down to the harbour with the village shop and 'The Hope and Anchor Inn'.

KINGSWEAR

Standing high up amongst a patchwork of narrow lanes and overlooking the Dart estuary is Kingswear. As well as the ferries across the river to Dartmouth (pictured below middle), there is also public transport via the Dart Valley Railway which originally opened in 1864 as part of the Great Western Railway.

The steam train chugs alongside the River Dart before arriving at the terminus in Kingswear (pictured below right).

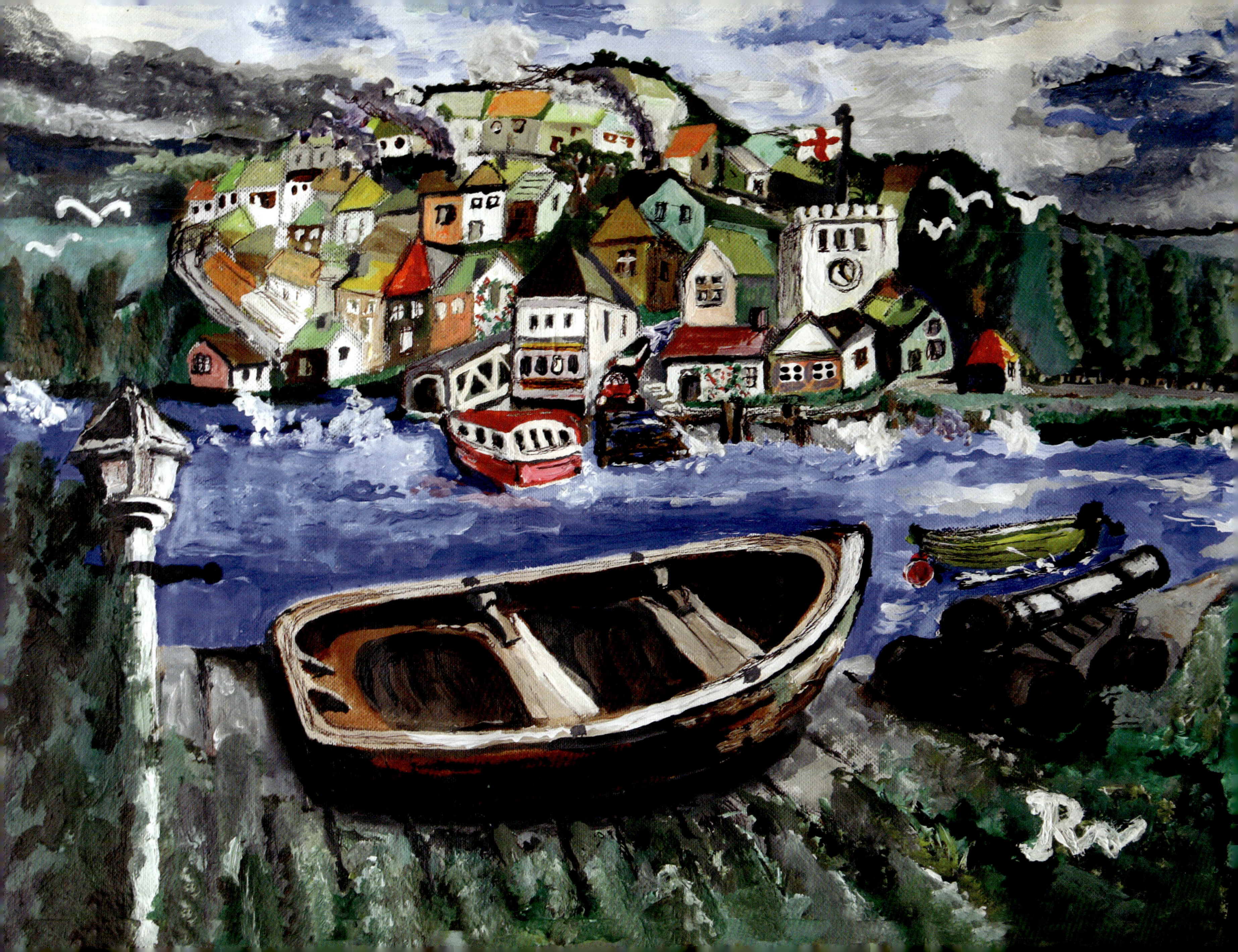
Rw

STOKE GABRIEL

Tucked away and nestling by the historic River Dart is the attractive and unspoilt village of Stoke Gabriel. History reveals that the village dates back to the 11th century.

Stoke Gabriel is a quintessential old English village with its 15th century church of St Mary and St Gabriel. In the churchyard (pictured below right) stands the famous yew tree which is reputed to be one of the oldest trees in England. Legend has it that if you walk backwards seven times round the tree you will be granted a wish.

Legends like this probably originated from an excess of liquid refreshment consumed in the Church House Inn (pictured below left) which, conveniently, is situated right next door to the church.

It is no wonder people say that Stoke Gabriel is 'the best kept secret in Devon'.

The West Country
NORTH DEVON

CLOVELLY

Clovelly in North Devon is one of the most beautiful villages in the world. What is especially unusual is that it is privately looked after and has been since Christine Hamlyn owned the estate in 1884 until her death in 1936.

The High Street – known as 'Up-a-long' and 'Down-a-long' is paved with pebbles. The steep narrow walkway (only reached by foot a quarter of a mile from the summit) leads down to a small harbour. On the way there is a pretty little fisherman's cottage showing how the Clovelly folk lived in the 18th century. Charles Kingsley, the famous author and poet, lived in the village in the 19th century.

Clovelly village and harbour are old enough to be recorded in the Doomsday Book 900 years ago. From Elizabethan days Clovelly relied upon its herring fishery and the large fishing fleet, protected by the rebuilt quay in 1826, continued to prosper in the 18th and 19th century (left picture below).

The present quay consists of massive stones with huge oak timber supports and ladders jutting out at the entrance of the harbour (middle picture below).

Thankfully today this beautiful village and harbour are still privately owned and both are handled with expert care and maintenance. Clovelly remains unspoilt and visitors treasure its peaceful atmosphere. It has been described as 'the old established beauty queen of England….an English Amalfi rising sheer from the bay.'

LYNMOUTH

This beautiful harbour of Lynmouth first came into the news when, in 1812, the poet Percy Bysshe Shelley used the village as a 'refuge'. Married to his 16 year old bride Mary, Shelley laid low avoiding the girl's threatening parents. Their hiding place was a little thatched cottage up the hill behind The Rising Sun Inn (pictured bottom left).

Lynmouth came into the news a second time when, in 1952, disaster struck overnight as the East and West Lyn rivers raged down narrow valleys. The floods caused devastation with cars and buildings being swept out to sea (pictured far right). Sadly 34 local folk lost their lives.

High up above Lynmouth Harbour at Waters Meet (pictured left), the rushing East Lyn River meets the Hoaroak Water. There are beautiful riverside walks and the National Trust had the sense to place a very welcome tea room half way down to the harbour.

One walk to definitely avoid is the 1-in-4 road up to Lynton. Instead visitors can take the cliff railway which climbs around 500ft along 862ft of track (pictured below left).

It is no wonder that famous poets like Wordsworth and Coleridge marvelled at the beauty of Lynmouth Harbour. Percy Bysshe Shelley would have loved to have stayed longer than just nine weeks, but, in the circumstances, it was wise to vacate to another refuge elsewhere.

APPLEDORE AND INSTOW

Situated opposite each other across the wide sandy estuary are the harbour villages of Appledore and Instow. The colour-washed cottages look out to where the two rivers, Taw and Torridge, meet in the estuary which is dotted with a colourful collection of boats.

Appledore is steeped in sea-faring history dating back to Anglo-Saxon times. Shipbuilding had been prevalent over hundreds of years. It is alleged that Elizabeth 1 granted 'free port' status when Appledore ships and sailors formed part of the fleet in the defeat of the Spanish Armada in 1588.

MORTEHOE

Sitting high up overlooking Woolacombe Bay and the charming Coombesgate Beach (pictured far left) is the small attractive village of Mortehoe. The little grey church of St Mary's at the top of the hill (pictured below left) has seen so many generations come and go. The church dates back to the 13th century and it has fine examples of a barrel roof and two Norman arches.

The treacherous nearby headland has claimed many victims. Five vessels were wrecked during the winter of 1852. 'Wreckers' operated along the coastline. These 'tricksters' lured the boats towards disaster with their lanterns of 'safety'. In the Scilly Isles there was a special prayer for wrecks.

'We pray thee, O Lord, not that wrecks should happen, but if they do, thou wilt guide them to the Scilly Isles for the benefit of our local poor people.'

39

WATER MOUTH COVE

This narrow inlet is a natural hideaway where sand and shingle spread to the harbour walls.

During the 2nd World War, Water Mouth was used to test 'Pluto' the 'pipeline under the ocean' that supplied the Allies with fuel after the D-Day invasion of Normandy. Watermouth Castle, built in 1825, overlooks the colourful yachts dotted around the cove below.

40

Wales

PEMBROKESHIRE

PORTHGAIN

For many years the granite cliffs of Porthgain were quarried for their stone which was crushed in the huge plant over the quay. The plant closed in 1932 and now there are only a few remains of what was a thriving industry . Porthgain must be one of the prettiest little harbours along the Pembrokeshire coastline.

Artist Alun Davies, and his Pyrenean mountain dog Sean, live in Porthgain where Alun has his cottage and gallery. The idyllic images of the picturesque harbour in summer are in strong contrast to Alun's painting of the ferocious winter storms which pound against the harbour walls (pictured left).

Today the harbour is an ideal location for pleasure craft and the local fishermen still set out to catch lobsters, crabs and assorted shellfish.

SOLVA

Tucked away in a winding creek between tall wooded hills, Solva resembles a little Cornish harbour.

There were many wrecks along the treacherous coast and in 1776 a lighthouse, built of wood in Solva, was towed out to sea and placed in position on a barge.

In those days there were only two lighthouse keepers and in 1801 one of them died in a freak accident. Fearing he might be accused of murder, the surviving keeper lashed the body to the gangway. But it took three months for the relief boat to arrive and by this time the keeper had gone mad. A minimum crew of three keepers was enforced following this tragedy.

Today, in less tragic and more tranquil times, Solva is a haven for sailing boats.

The village is dotted with neat colourful stone cottages some of which stand next to the clear running stream (pictured right).

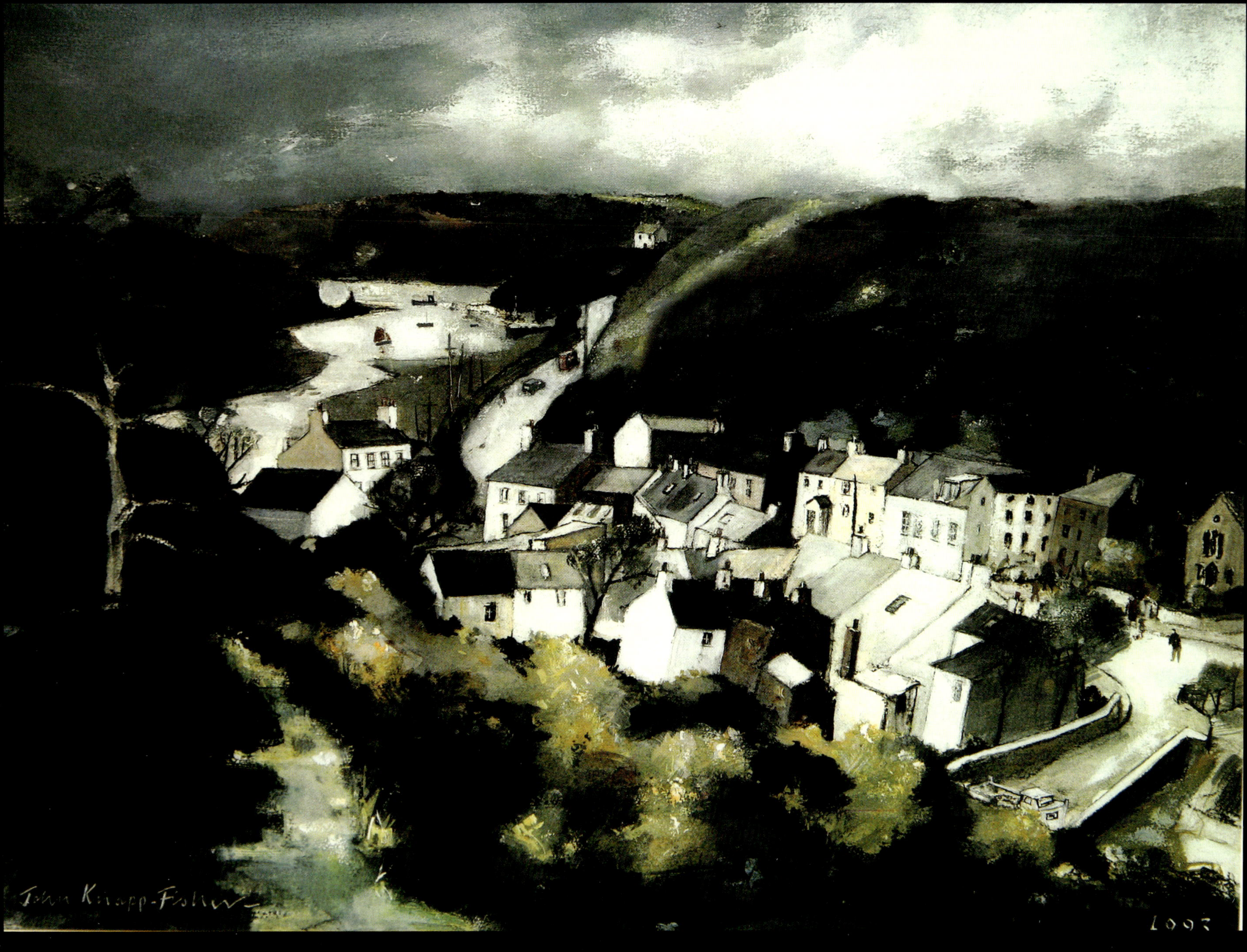
John Knapp-Fisher

ABEREIDDY

Once a busy harbour carved out in a slate quarry which closed in 1910, Abereiddy is well known for 'The Blue Lagoon' (pictures below). It was formed when the channel connecting the quarry to the sea was blasted, allowing the sea to flood in.

'The Blue Lagoon' is a very popular location for 'coasteering' – a water sports adventure including exhilarating 25 metre leaps into the water of similar depth below (pictured far right). The Mediterranean turquoise appearance of the water is deceptive because it is strikingly cold.

The narrow winding road to the little village of Abereiddy is bordered by attractive white stone cottages. Sadly only a few of these have survived and the well known local artist John Knapp-Fisher captured the bygone scene forty years ago in his painting 'Cottage No More' (opposite page).

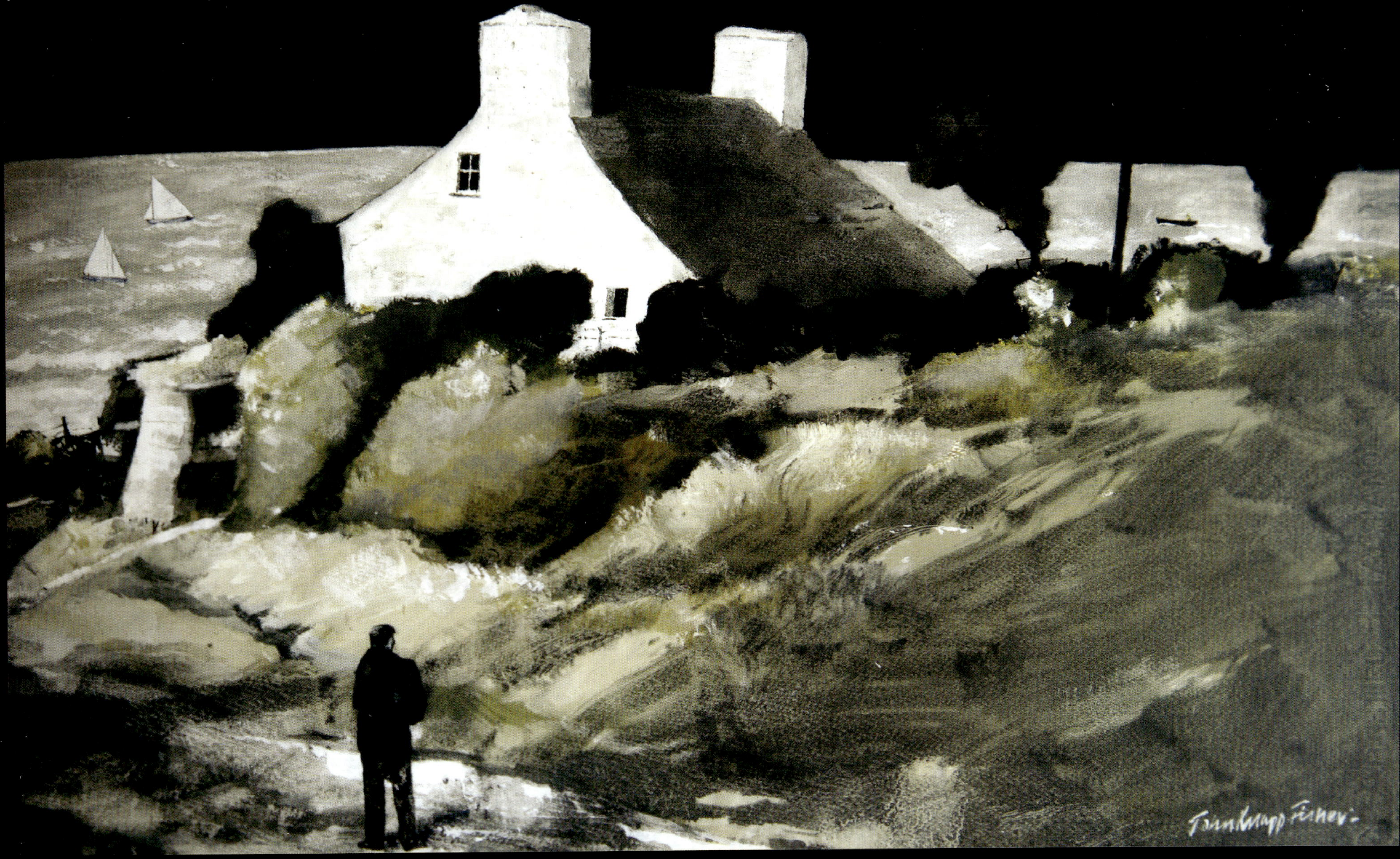

ST GOVAN'S CHAPEL
& THE HUNTSMAN'S LEAP

It is difficult to imagine a more strikingly minute chapel in all Britain. It is dramatically set tucked away deep down between precipitous cliffs.

St Govan was a 6th century hermit who established a cell for himself in this tiny hideaway amongst the rocks. The original cell was rebuilt in the 13th century when it was a place of pilgrimage for disabled people seeking a cure.

48

Just west of St Govan's Chapel is the Huntsman's Leap, so called because it was once jumped by a local huntsman. It is said that when he looked back and saw the hideousness of the chasm over which his horse had leaped (pictured below right), he dropped dead from fright.

THE OLD MILL AT TREVINE

It's hard to believe that less than 100 years ago this was a thriving hubbub of industry. For 500 years the mill was vital to life in Trevine. Villagers brought sacks of wheat to be milled into flour or bread.

The bay below the old mill was used for trading and fishing boats. Sea captains, quarrymen and fishermen lived in the white-stoned cottages (pictured below right).

By 1900 cheap grain from overseas was being milled by much larger mills in towns. This led to the end of local mills like this one and sadly Trevine mill closed in 1918. Today all that remains lying in the derelict mill are the grinding stones (pictured below left).

The Welsh poet William Crwys Williams, sensing the death knoll sound of what was then the centre of the community, wrote –

'The mill is not grinding corn tonight
In Trevine on the edge of the sea.'

North England

NORTHUMBERLAND
& NORTH YORKSHIRE

BAMBURGH

Bamburgh is one of England's most majestic castles. It was first fortified by the early Kings of Northumbria and stands 150 feet above the sandy bay surrounded by 8 acres of dunes.

The castle towers above the tucked away village of Bamburgh which has a row of pretty 18th century cottages around a little green (pictured right).

BAMBURGH

L·N·E·R   Illustrated Booklets describing the territory served by the Company
Free at all Enquiry Offices   **L·N·E·R**

THE HOLY ISLAND OF LINDISFARNE

The little village on Holy Island is made up of attractive rose-clad cottages. With only two hundred or so inhabitants, the village is indeed a 'hidey-hole' sanctuary. Lindisfarne Castle (now owned by The National Trust) casts a romantic backcloth to the once thriving fishing harbour. But the decline of the herring fleet is evident in the hulks of the old storage boats cut in half and lying upturned.

Lindisfarne became a Holy Island for a second time in 1013 when building began on the Norman Priory whose ruins still stand today (pictured below).

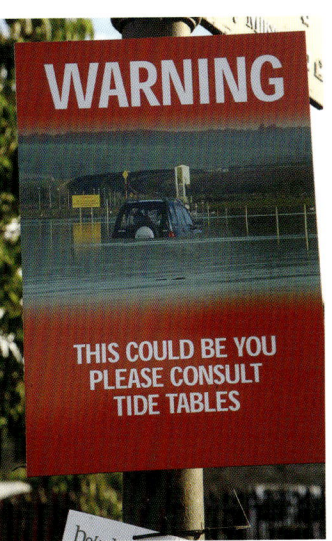

Beyond the harbour, perched on the great crag on Holy Island is Lindisfarne Castle. Surprisingly it was not fortified until 1542 when gun-posts were set up to defend the harbour against the marauding Scots.

In 1819 the guns were removed (after never having to fire a shot in anger) and the castle sadly fell into disuse. Happily it was recreated by the architect Edwin Lutyens in 1902.

For up to 11 out of every 24 hours, the sea cuts Holy Island off from the mainland. Both locals and visitors are controlled by the tides and timetables plus warning signs are clearly displayed at the edge of the causeway (pictured below right). It's almost a mile across so woe 'betide' if a driver is caught halfway.

CRASTER & DUNSTANBURGH CASTLE

Craster is an unspoiled fishing village. Many of the houses are built of hard dark stone. Once a busy harbour, today there are only a few boats that go out for lobsters and crabs.

Craster is famous for its kippers which are smoked above the little harbour (pictured far right). The smokehouses of L.Robson & Sons are very much in business and they still smoke in the traditional way over fires of oak sawdust.

Today the renowned Craster kippers are purchased throughout the UK and Europe.

The only way to reach the ruins of Dunstanburgh Castle is on foot along the exhilarating coastal path from the little harbour of Craster.

The castle was built by Thomas Earl of Lancaster in 1313. Little of the castle remains and fragments of the huge gatehouse protrude towards the skies like giant chess pieces.

The relics of the ruined walls, once several feet thick, are evidence of the sieges that bludgeoned Dunstanburgh Castle during The Wars of the Roses.

ROBIN HOOD'S BAY
NORTH YORKSHIRE

Known locally as 'Bay Town', there are dubious links with the Sherwood Forest outlaw. One legend is that Robin Hood came to Whitby to help the Abbot to beat off Danish invaders.

Tiny fishermen's cottages line the cobbled twisting alleyways which lead down to the sea.

Sadly, in 1975, erosion caused several cottages to topple into the sea. As a result a 40ft high sea-wall was built to protect the village.

Smuggling was at its height in the 18th century and Robin Hood's Bay was no exception to the thievery to beat the revenue men. The smugglers devised a cunning scheme to transport their contraband by using a large tunnel on the harbour front (pictured left). This lengthy tunnel led its way to the safety of a manor house high up behind the village.

Today, in the garden of this 18th century manor house (pictured below), a large hole is evident through which the smugglers transferred the contraband up from the harbour tunnel. The Lord's of the manor were more than happy to collaborate with the smugglers – but at a price!

STAITHES

With its winding colourful streets and higgledypiggledy cottages, Staithes has the air of a place lost in time. Set deep in a gorge, a cluster of card-like houses are perched overlooking the river below.

Once one of the largest fishing ports on the Northeast coast, the small compact harbour is now home only to a few brightly coloured boats (some known as 'Whitby Cobles'). Today the local fishermen go to sea in search of cod, lobsters and crabs.

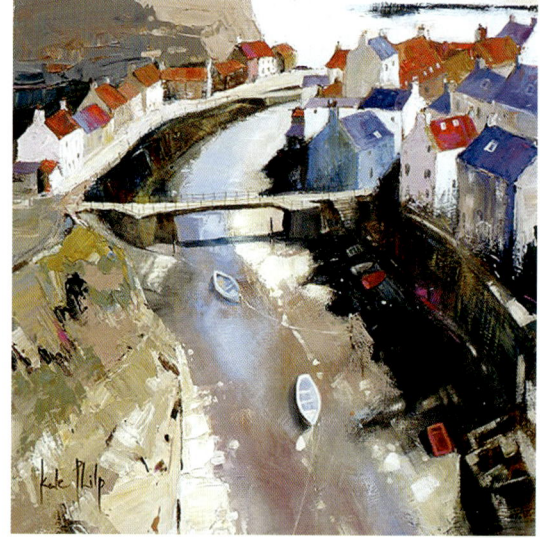

In 1744 one of the world's greatest explorers spent his youth in the harbour of Staithes. At the age of 16, James Cook (pictured below) worked as an apprentice to William Sanderson, a haberdasher in the village. Very soon Cook felt the urge to go to sea and joined the Royal Navy. This was the start of the many historic explorations he made around the world.

Today the comforting feature about Staithes is that the charm and character will never change and it will always remain to be a unique and eyecatching coastal 'Hidey-Hole'.

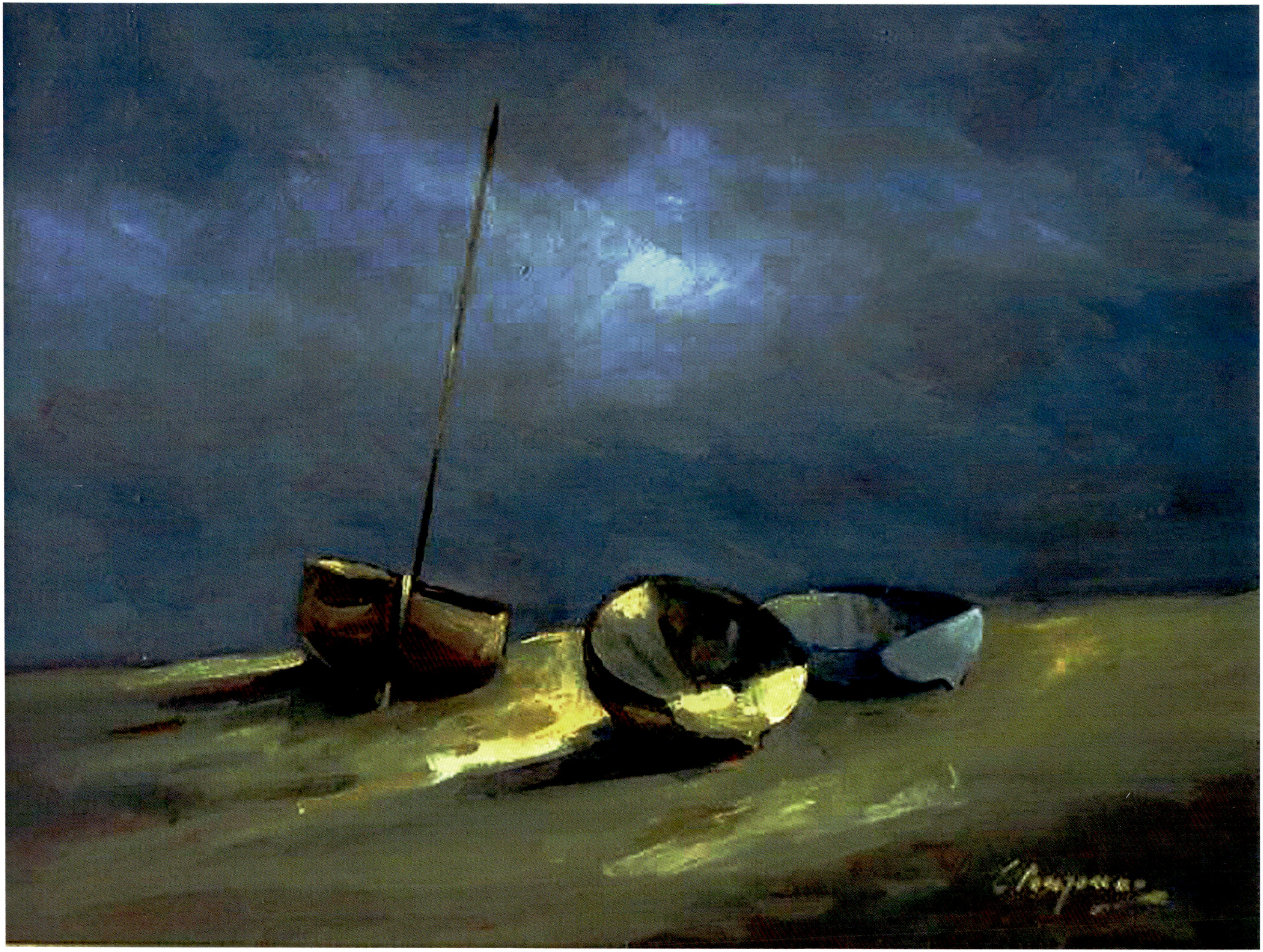

East Anglia

NORFOLK

BLAKENEY

The diminutive sailing village of Blakeney lies at the end of a channel which almost dries up at low tide. The main high street runs down a narrow slope to the harbour. On either side are picturesque white cottages with colourful doors and window frames (pictured below right).

The village of Blakeney was originally called 'Snitterley' but, long ago, it was engulfed by the sea and lost forever. In 1953 the East Anglian coast suffered from disastrous floods and the village was under six feet of sea water.

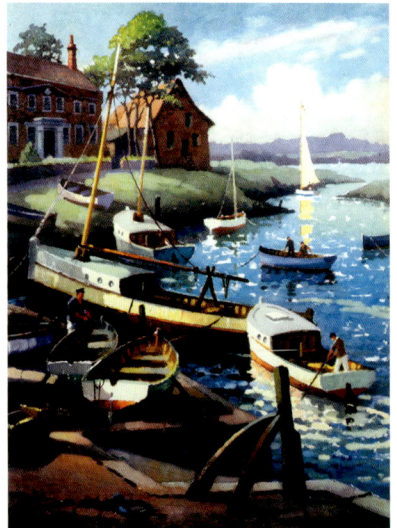

64

Just north of the village is Blakeney Point, a nature reserve since 1912. It is now owned by The National Trust.

Not only do thousands of terns nest there during May and July but there is a colony of seals enjoying themselves on the sands.

HOLKHAM HALL

Just inland from Holkham Bay is the vast magnificent Palladian mansion of Holkham Hall designed for Thomas Coke, Earl of Leicester in 1730. Inside there are beautifully furnished rooms and paintings by Van Dyck, Rubens and other masters. Within the amplitude of parkland is a lake, a walled garden and a museum of bygones featuring classic motor vehicles (pictured far right).

Close to Holkham Beach (pictured left) and situated on the edge of the Holkham Estate is the diminutive village of Burnham Thorpe. There are other villages with the Burnham name (such as Burnham Staithe) in close proximity of each other and these are known as the 'Seven Burnhams'.

But the most famous of the Burnhams is Burnham Thorpe for this was Lord Horatio Nelson's birthplace. The old rectory where he was born in 1758 was pulled down in 1802 but All Saints' Church has the font where he was christened. Also close by in the chancel is a bust of Nelson.

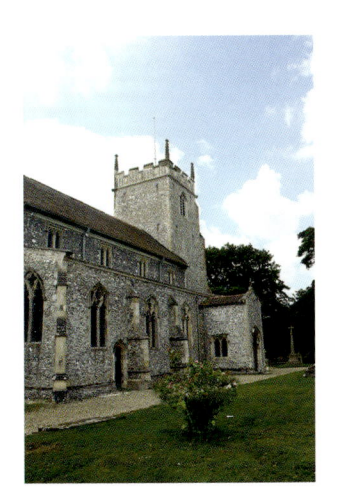

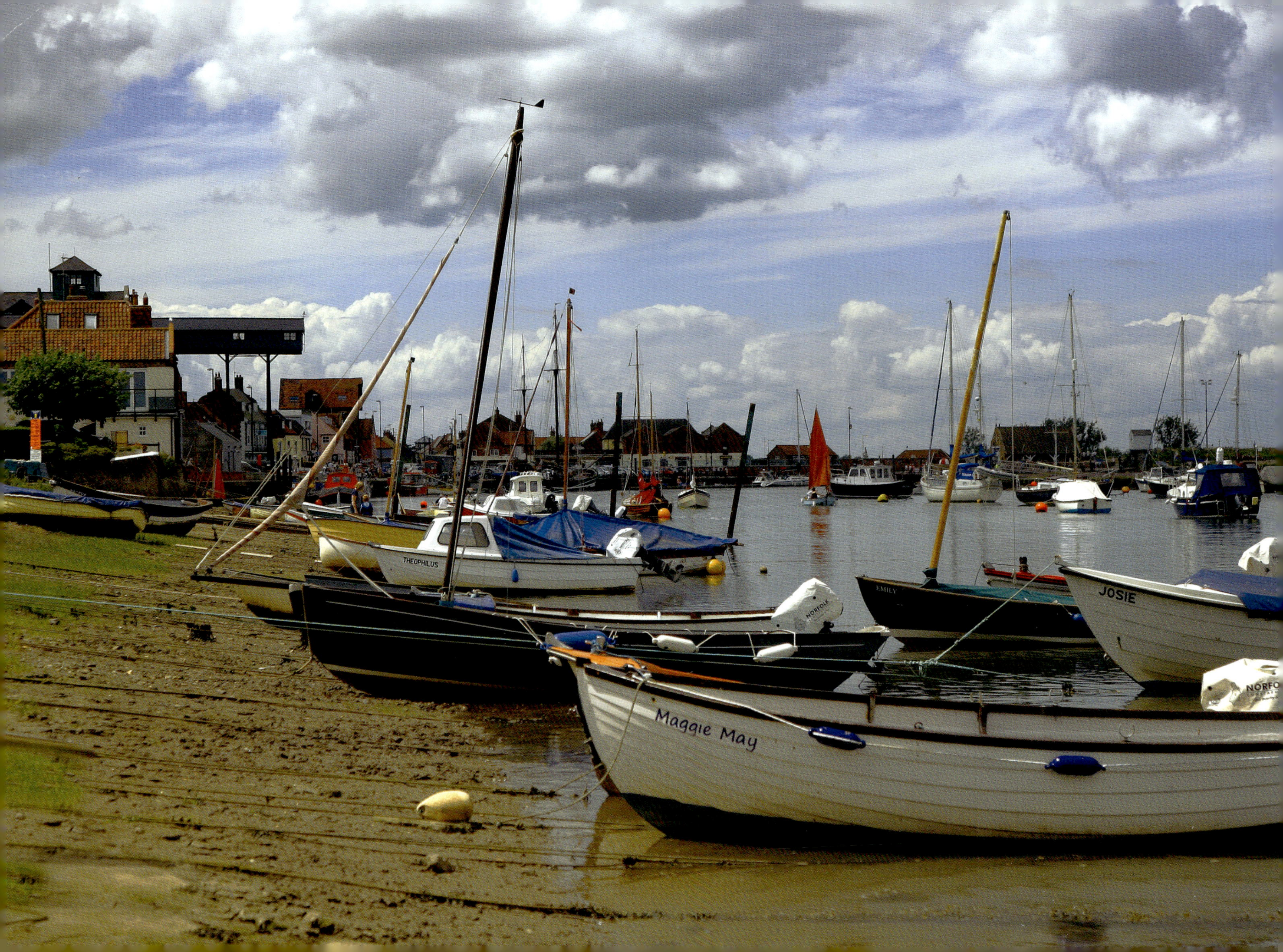
THEOPHILUS
JOSIE
Maggie May

WELLS-NEXT-THE-SEA

Wells consists of really just three parts – the quayside, the narrow lanes behind it and the beach which is only a mile away to the north of the village.

The quayside at Wells is a dream for both visitors and locals who love to eat fish. Fresh out of the trawlers the daily catch is hauled straight onto the quayside where several stalls are buzzing selling dressed crabs, mussels, cockles and samphire (a Norfolk speciality).

The quayside is a haven for a vast array of boats of all shapes and sizes. Together with the fishing trawlers, motor boats and an old attractive barge with its high mast are moored alongside the quay (pictured below left).

Just outside the village is the Wells-Walsingham Railway (pictured below). The line opened in 1982 and the well-preserved colourful steam train travels with its attractive small carriages the four miles to and fro the 30 minute ride between the two villages.

69

CLEY-NEXT-THE-SEA

As far back as the middle ages Cley was a busy fishing port, but, like much of the Norfolk coastline, the sea receded which resulted in vast expanses of marshland. Today the Cley Marshes is a 650 acre nature reserve where terns, larks and many wildfowl breed in winter.

The attractive village, with a well-known pottery shop and art galleries, has tiny narrow streets. Overlooking them is the 18th century tower windmill standing majestically on the edge of the marsh (pictured below).

ARTIST'S ACKNOWLEDGEMENTS

Cornwall: Oliver Bedford LRIBA, BWS, SGA 1902-1977 – Mousehole, Veryan, Cadgwith, Gorran Haven & Polperro
                      Ernest Procter – Porthgwarra (by permission of the Penlee Art Gallery)
                      Brett Humphries – Polperro
                      R.Scaddon – 'Dolly Portreath' (by permission of the Penlee Art Gallery)
                      Josff Bullen Photo Collection – Botallack Mine
                      Richard Tuff – Beside The Wave, Falmouth, Cadgwith, Helford & Flushing Pier
                      Keith Geddes – Polperro (pictured below) & Bryony Hill—The Ship Inn, Mousehole.

East Anglia: Michael Chapman – Norfolk Boats Brian Ryder ROIIEA – Holkham Beach & Cley-Next-The-Sea

North Devon: Mark Woolacott – Instow Boats, Lynmouth Harbour & Watermouth Cove Roger Whitburn – Clovelly

South Devon: Brett Humphries – Hope Cove Roger Whitburn – Kingswear

Northumberland: Kate Van Suddese – Bamburgh Castle Pam Vardy – Lindisfarne Castle Mick Oxley – Dunstanburgh Coastline
                      Kate Philp – Staithes

Wales: John Knapp – Fisher Abereiddy & Solva
                      Alun Davies – Porthgain

North Yorkshire: Captain James Cook – National Maritime Museum.

FURTHER ACKNOWLEDGEMENTS
& SPECIAL THANKS

Further Acknowledgements: Holkham Hall, Norfolk: By kind permission of Viscount Coke and the Trustees of the Holkham Estate.

LNER Railway Posters: Courtesy of The Science & Society Picture Gallery.

National Trust Organization Properties:- Cornwall – Mullion Cove, Boscastle, Mousehole, Penberth Cove and Cape Cornwall. Devon: Greenway House, Lynmouth. Northumberland: Lindisfarne, Holy Island, Dunstanburgh Castle. Norfolk: Blakeney Point. Yorkshire: Robin Hood's Bay

Special Thanks: Jasmine Rodgers @ Science & Society Picture Gallery, London. Emma Bushell @ Holkham Estate, Norfolk. The Penlee Art Gallery, Penzance. Beside The Wave Gallery, Falmouth & artist Richard Tuff (Helford pictured below). National Maritime Museum – Captain James Cook.

David Russell & Jane McGovern at Russells Photo Imaging, Wimbledon.

Val Lanceley who initially sparked the idea of involving local artists in the book.

Very Special Thanks: Sue Harden for all her continuous support and for her technical wizardry and marketing skills. Thanks as well to David Hughes for all his help as my Welsh 'Sherpa' introducing me to many beautiful 'Hidey Holes' along the Pembrokeshire Coastline. My sincere gratitude to Zane who, with an abundance of patience, finally managed to put the book to bed.

Rosie Grindrod at Troubador Publishing Ltd. and, finally to all my family who, once again, were always so supportive.

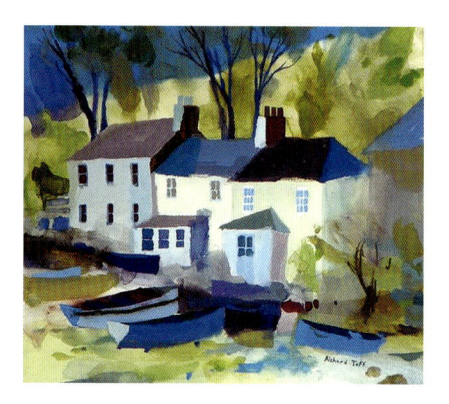